No part of this book may be reproduced, distributed, or transmitted in any form or by any means, including photocopying, recording, or other electronic or mechanical methods, without the prior written permission of the publisher.

Culture lover is the copyright owner of the content of this book and does not authorize the use of the content of this book by any other person or entity. The use of the content of this book without permission will constitute a copyright infringement, and Culture lover has the right to take legal action for copyright infringement.

Copyright © 2025 Culture lover
All rights reserved.

CONTENTS

1. Introduction to Japan (4)
2. Daily Life Fun Facts (12)
3. Famous Landmarks (24)
4. Cultural Traditions (37)
5. Food and Cuisine (47)
6. Festivals and Celebrations (56)
7. Amazing Animals of Japan (68)
8. Cool Japanese Inventions (77)

INTRODUCTION TO JAPAN

Tokyo, JAPAN

Introduction to Japan

Japan is made up of over 6,800 islands! The four main islands are Hokkaido, Honshu, Shikoku, and Kyushu. Imagine living on an island paradise!

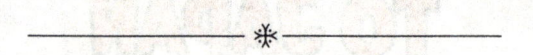

---- ❈ ----

Japan is often called the "Land of the Rising Sun." This name comes from the Japanese words for Japan, which mean "sun origin." It's like the sun says hello to Japan first every morning!

---- ❈ ----

Mount Fuji is Japan's highest mountain and an active volcano. It's a symbol of Japan and a popular place to visit. Climbing Mount Fuji is like reaching the top of the world!

Introduction to Japan

Japan's history is very old, starting thousands of years ago. The first people in Japan were hunters and gatherers. They made pottery and used stone tools.

Samurai were ancient Japanese warriors who followed a code of honor called Bushido. They were skilled fighters and protected their lords. Imagine being a brave samurai with a shiny sword!

Every spring, Japan celebrates the blooming of cherry blossom trees. This is called Hanami, which means "flower viewing." People have picnics under the pink and white flowers.

Introduction to Japan

The Japanese tea ceremony is a special way to make and serve tea. It's about being calm and peaceful. People learn to do it slowly and carefully, like a relaxing dance.

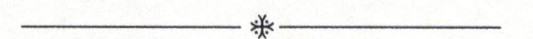

---   ❈   ---

Sushi is a famous Japanese food made with rice and fish. It comes in many shapes and sizes, like rolls and bites. Eating sushi is like having a yummy fish picnic!

---   ❈   ---

Ramen is a popular Japanese noodle soup. It comes with different toppings like meat and veggies. Slurping ramen is fun and tasty, like a warm hug in a bowl!

Introduction to Japan

Origami is the art of folding paper into shapes. You can make animals, flowers, and more. It's like creating magic with just a piece of paper!

Japan has some of the most advanced toilets in the world. They have buttons for music, heated seats, and more. Using a high-tech toilet is like sitting on a fancy throne!

Japan is filled with vending machines that offer a wide range of items, from beverages to toys. They are practically everywhere, making it feel like there's a mini-store on every corner!

Introduction to Japan

Bullet trains, or Shinkansen, are super fast trains in Japan. They can go over 200 miles per hour! Riding a bullet train is like zooming through the countryside on a speedy rocket!

———————— ❋ ————————

Sumo is a traditional Japanese sport where big wrestlers try to push each other out of a ring. It's like a fun and exciting game of king of the hill.

———————— ❋ ————————

Kimonos are traditional Japanese clothes that are colorful and beautiful. People wear them for special events. It's like dressing up in a fancy and pretty outfit!

Introduction to Japan

Bonsai trees are tiny and cute. They are grown in small pots and trimmed to stay small. It's like having a miniature forest in your home!

Haiku is a type of Japanese poetry with three lines. It's about nature and feelings. Writing haiku is like creating a short and sweet poem!

Kawaii means "cute" in Japanese. It's a big part of Japanese culture, from toys to fashion. Everything can be kawaii, like a world full of cuteness!

Introduction to Japan

Futons are traditional Japanese beds that roll up during the day. They are comfortable and easy to store. Sleeping on a futon is like camping indoors!

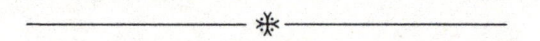

Chopsticks are used to eat food in Japan. They come in different sizes and materials. Using chopsticks is like playing a fun game with your food!

Japan has many festivals with music, dance, and food. They celebrate seasons, history, and culture. Going to a festival is like having a big party with friends!

DAILY LIFE FUN FACTS

Daily Life Fun Facts

In Japan, many people start their day with a warm bowl of miso soup. It's like having a cozy hug to wake you up!

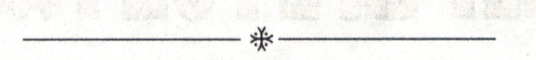

---------------- ❈ ----------------

Most students in Japan wear uniforms to school. They have special sailor-style uniforms for girls and military-style uniforms for boys. Imagine everyone looking neat and tidy!

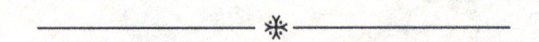

---------------- ❈ ----------------

Kids bring bento boxes to school for lunch. These are like little lunchboxes filled with yummy food, often decorated to look cute and fun.

Daily Life Fun Facts

Convenience stores, or "konbini," are very popular in Japan. They sell everything from food to magazines. It's like a one-stop shop for all your needs!

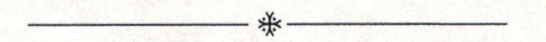

---- ❋ ----

Bikes are a common way to get around in Japan. People use them for short trips to the store or to visit friends. Imagine riding your bike through bustling city streets!

---- ❋ ----

In Japan, respect for elders is very important. Kids learn to bow and use polite language with older people. It's like showing extra kindness to grandparents and teachers!

Daily Life Fun Facts

Japanese culture values group harmony. People work together and help each other out. It's like being part of a big, friendly team!

---------- ❋ ----------

In spring, people gather with family and friends for picnics under cherry blossom trees. They bring delicious food and cozy blankets, enjoying the stunning blossoms. It feels like a celebration in a magical pink and white world!

---------- ❋ ----------

Rice is a big part of Japanese meals. People eat it with almost every dish, from breakfast to dinner. Imagine having a yummy bowl of rice with every meal!

Daily Life Fun Facts

Japan has many earthquakes, so people are always prepared. Schools and homes have earthquake drills and safety plans. It's like being ready for any adventure!

---❄---

Japanese people love giving gifts. They wrap them beautifully and present them with both hands. It's like making every gift extra special!

---❄---

New Year is a big deal in Japan. People eat special foods, visit shrines, and send greeting cards to friends. It's like a huge and happy holiday party!

Daily Life Fun Facts

In autumn, people in Japan have moon-viewing parties. They admire the full moon and enjoy seasonal foods. It's like having a magical night under the moonlight!

---- ❋ ----

In winter, families gather to eat hot pots together. They cook meat and vegetables in a big pot at the table. It's like having a warm, cozy feast!

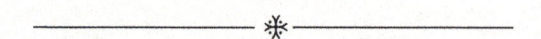

---- ❋ ----

In Japan, people do a big spring cleaning to welcome the new season. They clean their homes from top to bottom. It's like giving your house a fresh start!

Daily Life Fun Facts

Bamboo is used to make many things in Japan, like baskets and fences. It's a strong and flexible plant. Imagine creating cool things with bamboo!

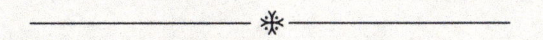

---- ❄ ----

Paper lanterns are a popular decoration in Japan. They come in many shapes and colors and are often seen at festivals. It's like having a glowing, colorful party!

---- ❄ ----

During the Obon festival, people light lanterns and float them on rivers. It's a way to honor and remember their ancestors. Imagine a peaceful, glowing river parade!

Daily Life Fun Facts

Shichi-Go-San is a festival for children aged 3, 5, and 7. They dress up in traditional clothes and visit shrines to pray for good health. It's like having a special day just for kids!

---- ❈ ----

In January, young people celebrate Coming of Age Day. They turn 20 and are officially recognized as adults. It's like having a big birthday party with friends!

---- ❈ ----

Japanese people have a deep respect for nature. They enjoy outdoor activities like hiking and picnics. It's like being friends with the natural world!

Daily Life Fun Facts

Many people in Japan study the art of the tea ceremony. They practice preparing and serving tea with grace and calmness. It's like mastering a peaceful and elegant dance!

Japanese people learn calligraphy, which is beautiful writing with a brush and ink. They write poems and words in a fancy way. It's like making art with letters!

Martial arts like judo and karate are popular in Japan. People practice them to stay fit and learn self-defense. It's like being a strong and skilled warrior!

Daily Life Fun Facts

Karaoke is a favorite pastime in Japan. People sing their favorite songs with friends at karaoke bars. It's like having a big, fun singing party!

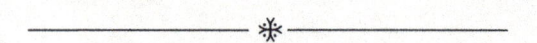

Video game arcades are popular hangouts in Japan. People play all kinds of games, from racing to dancing. It's like stepping into a world of endless fun and adventure!

Many schools in Japan start the day with morning exercises. Students gather in the schoolyard to do stretches and warm-ups together. It's like having a mini sports day every morning!

Daily Life Fun Facts

Students in Japan help clean their classrooms and school grounds after classes. They sweep, mop, and even clean the toilets. It's like being part of a big cleaning team!

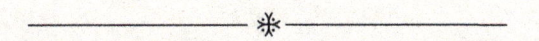

Many train stations in Japan have lockers for storing bags. They are useful for travelers and shoppers. It's like having your own storage space in the city!

Japanese people highly respect punctuality. Trains, buses, and meetings almost always begin as scheduled. It's like living in a world where everyone is always on time!

Daily Life Fun Facts

In some Japanese zoos, polar bears get frozen fish popsicles in summer to cool off. Yummy and refreshing!

In Japan, people take off their shoes before entering a house. They wear special indoor slippers. But don't wear them in the bathroom—there are separate bathroom slippers!

In Japan, you don't tip at restaurants or taxis. Great service is expected, and tipping can even be considered rude. Keep your coins!

FAMOUS LANDMARKS

Famous Landmarks

Mount Fuji is the highest mountain in Japan. It is shaped like a perfect cone. Many people climb it to see the sunrise from the top.

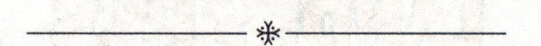

The Tokyo Tower is a tall red and white tower. It looks like the Eiffel Tower in Paris. You can go up to the top for a great view of the city.

The Tokyo Skytree is even taller than the Tokyo Tower. It has a special design to withstand earthquakes. You can see all of Tokyo from the observation deck.

Famous Landmarks

Kinkaku-ji is a beautiful golden temple in Kyoto. It is covered in real gold leaf. The temple is surrounded by a lovely garden and pond.

Fushimi Inari Shrine has thousands of red gates. They form a long tunnel you can walk through. Each gate is a gift from someone who made a wish.

Himeji Castle is a big white castle in Japan. It is also called the White Heron Castle. It has many towers and walls to explore.

Famous Landmarks

Osaka Castle is a famous castle in Osaka. It has a big park around it. You can learn about Japanese history inside the castle.

---- ✼ ----

Kiyomizu-dera is a temple in Kyoto with a big wooden stage. You can see the whole city from the stage. It is especially beautiful in the fall with colorful leaves.

---- ✼ ----

Senso-ji Temple, located in Tokyo, is renowned for its large red lantern and holds the distinction of being the city's oldest temple. A bustling street lined with shops leads up to the temple.

Famous Landmarks

Itsukushima Shrine is on an island called Miyajima. It is partly built over the water. At high tide, it looks like it is floating on the sea.

Shibuya Crossing is a famous intersection in Tokyo. Many people cross the street at the same time. It is one of the busiest crossings in the world.

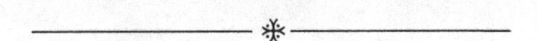

Meiji Shrine is a peaceful place in Tokyo. It is surrounded by a big forest. You can write your wishes on wooden tablets and hang them up.

Famous Landmarks

The Arashiyama Bamboo Grove is a forest of tall bamboo. It is in Kyoto and is very quiet. You can walk through the grove and listen to the bamboo swaying.

Nijo Castle is in Kyoto and has special floors. They squeak like birds when you walk on them. This was a security system to protect the castle.

Todaiji Temple is in Nara and has a big Buddha statue. It is one of the largest bronze statues in the world. The temple is in a park with friendly deer.

Famous Landmarks

Nara Park is famous for its friendly deer. They walk around the park and bow to you. You can feed them special deer crackers.

The Hakone Open-Air Museum is a big park with art. You can see sculptures and play on the grass. There is even a hot spring foot bath.

Nikko Toshogu Shrine is a colorful shrine in Nikko. It has many carvings and decorations. You can see monkeys and other animals in the carvings.

Famous Landmarks

Matsumoto Castle is a black castle in the mountains. It is also called the Crow Castle. You can explore the inside and see old weapons.

Kumano Kodo is a long trail in the mountains. It leads to special shrines. People walk the trail to visit the shrines and enjoy nature.

Akihabara is a fun place in Tokyo with many shops. You can find toys, games, and electronics. It is also called Electric Town.

Famous Landmarks

Tsukiji Fish Market is a big market in Tokyo. You can see many kinds of fish and seafood. There are also restaurants where you can eat fresh sushi.

--- ❋ ---

Odaiba is a man-made island in Tokyo Bay. It has big shopping malls and a Ferris wheel. You can see the rainbow bridge and the Statue of Liberty.

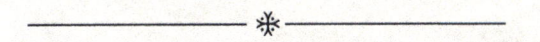

--- ❋ ---

Ueno Park is a big park in Tokyo with a zoo. You can see pandas and other animals. There are also museums and a big pond with boats.

Famous Landmarks

Asakusa is an old part of Tokyo with many temples. You can see the big red lantern at Senso-ji Temple. There are also many shops with traditional snacks.

---❋---

Shinjuku Gyoen is a big garden in Tokyo. It has many kinds of trees and flowers. You can see cherry blossoms in the spring and colorful leaves in the fall.

---❋---

Yoyogi Park is a big park in Tokyo with lots of space to play. You can see people dancing, playing music, and having picnics. There are also big festivals in the park.

Famous Landmarks

Fukui Station is a big train station in Fukui. It has many shops and restaurants. You can also see the Fukui Prefectural Dinosaur Museum and the Eiheiji Temple.

Chiba Station is a big train station in Chiba. It has many shops and restaurants. You can also see the Chiba Castle and the Chiba Zoological Park.

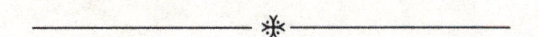

Kawaguchiko Lake is a beautiful lake near Mount Fuji. You can take a boat ride on the lake. There are also many swans and other birds to see.

Famous Landmarks

Chureito Pagoda is a tall tower near Mount Fuji. It has many levels and is very colorful. You can see Mount Fuji and the city from the top.

Nagasaki Peace Park is a place to remember World War II. It has a big statue of a man pointing to the sky. The statue stands for peace and hope for the future.

Hakone Onsen is a town with many hot springs. You can soak in the warm water and relax. There are also many hotels and shops to visit.

Famous Landmarks

Kanazawa Castle is a big castle in Kanazawa. It has many towers and walls to explore. You can also see a beautiful garden next to the castle.

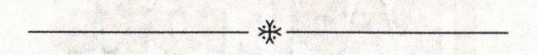

Kenrokuen Garden is a famous garden in Kanazawa. It has many kinds of trees and flowers. You can see cherry blossoms in the spring and colorful leaves in the fall.

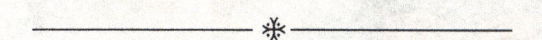

Zojoji Temple is a big temple in Tokyo. It has a big gate with two statues. You can see the Tokyo Tower from the temple.

CULTURAL TRADITIONS

Cultural Traditions

The tea ceremony in Japan, known as chanoyu or chado, is a unique ritual for serving tea. It involves preparing and enjoying tea in a slow and mindful manner.

The Cherry Blossom Festival is a big event in Japan. It happens in the spring when cherry trees bloom. People have picnics under the trees and enjoy the pink flowers.

Calligraphy is the art of writing beautifully in Japan. It is done with a brush and ink. You can write poems, letters, and more.

Cultural Traditions

Ikebana is the art of arranging flowers in Japan. It is a way to appreciate nature and beauty. You can make beautiful displays with flowers and plants.

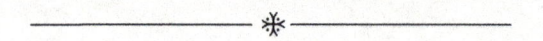

———————— ✽ ————————

Kabuki is a traditional type of theater in Japan. Actors wear fancy costumes and makeup. They tell stories with singing, dancing, and acting.

———————— ✽ ————————

Tsukimi is a tradition of looking at the full moon. It happens in the fall in Japan. People eat special rice cakes and enjoy the moonlight.

Cultural Traditions

Girls' Day is a holiday for girls in Japan. It happens on March 3rd. Families display dolls and wish for their daughters' happiness.

Boys' Day is a holiday for boys in Japan. It happens on May 5th. Families fly carp-shaped windsocks and wish for their sons' strength.

Fukubukuro are lucky bags sold in Japan. They are sold at the start of the year. You can find them in stores with surprise items inside.

Cultural Traditions

Temple visits are also a important part of Japanese culture. People go to temples to pray and meditate. They also light incense and make offerings.

Kakizome is a tradition of writing wishes on paper. It happens in January in Japan. People write their wishes and then burn the paper.

Setsubun is a festival to celebrate the start of spring. It happens in February in Japan. People throw beans to chase away bad luck.

Cultural Traditions

Japanese gardens are beautiful and calm. They have plants, rocks, and water features. You can walk through them and relax.

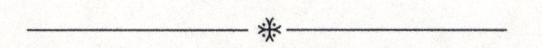

---※---

Bamboo is a strong and flexible plant in Japan. It is used in many things like buildings, furniture, and even food. You can make flutes and other instruments with it.

---※---

The Japanese language is unique and has three writing systems. They are hiragana, katakana, and kanji. You can learn to read and write them with practice.

Cultural Traditions

Japanese temples are peaceful and quiet. People go there to pray and meditate. They also light incense and make offerings.

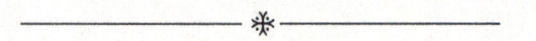

Obi is the wide belt that's tied around a kimono. Tying it is an art all by itself! Some obi designs are so fancy they look like pieces of art.

Geta are wooden sandals often worn with traditional clothing. They make a funny clacking sound when you walk. It's like having music in your footsteps!

Cultural Traditions

Samurai once wore armor that was beautifully crafted. These warriors were not only brave but also stylish! Their swords, called katanas, were masterpieces of craftsmanship.

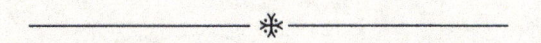

---- ❇ ----

Japanese pottery, like tea bowls, is famous for its simple beauty. Some pieces are so special they're treated like treasures. Drinking tea from them feels extra fancy!

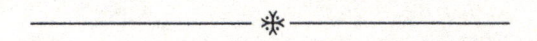

---- ❇ ----

At home, people often sit on cushions called zabuton instead of chairs. It's comfy and keeps you close to the floor. Plus, it makes meals feel more relaxed.

Cultural Traditions

Many Japanese homes have a small shrine called a kamidana. It's a place to pray and show respect to spirits. It's like having a mini temple at home.

―――――― ✳ ――――――

Bowing is a big part of Japanese culture. People bow to say hello, goodbye, or thank you. The deeper the bow, the more respect you show.

―――――― ✳ ――――――

Japanese people often say "Itadakimasu" before eating. It means "I humbly receive" and is a way to show gratitude for the food. It's like saying thank you to everyone who made the meal possible.

Cultural Traditions

Onsen, or hot springs, are a favorite way to relax in Japan. People soak in natural, warm water surrounded by beautiful scenery. It's like a spa day in nature!

---- ❄ ----

In Japan, people give gifts wrapped beautifully with colorful paper and ribbons. They believe the way you wrap a gift is as important as the gift itself. It's like sharing love and care through wrapping!

---- ❄ ----

In Japan, people cherish the tradition of enjoying seasonal foods. During the summer, they savor refreshing dishes like cold noodles, while winter offers the comfort of warm hotpots. It's as if each season is honored through its distinctive culinary offerings!

FOOD AND CUISINE

Food and Cuisine

Sushi is a famous food from Japan. It is made with rice, fish, and vegetables. You can eat it with chopsticks and soy sauce.

Ramen is a beloved soup dish in Japan, featuring a combination of noodles, meat, and vegetables. It is widely available in numerous restaurants and shops across the country.

Tempura is fried seafood and vegetables. It is light and crispy. You can eat it with a special sauce.

Food and Cuisine

Sashimi is raw fish sliced thinly. It is very fresh and tasty. You can eat it with soy sauce and wasabi.

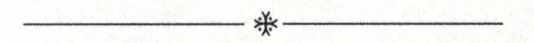

Miso soup is a traditional soup in Japan. It is made with miso paste and dashi broth. You can add tofu and green onions too.

Onigiri are rice balls with fillings. They are a popular snack in Japan. You can find them in convenience stores and make them at home.

Food and Cuisine

Yakitori are grilled skewers of meat. They are a popular street food in Japan. You can find them at festivals and markets.

Takoyaki are fried balls of batter with octopus inside. They are a popular snack in Japan. You can eat them with special sauces.

Okonomiyaki is a savory pancake. It is made with cabbage, meat, and other ingredients. You can find it in restaurants and make it at home.

Food and Cuisine

Tonkatsu is a breaded and fried pork cutlet. It is a popular dish in Japan. You can eat it with special sauces and cabbage.

--- ❈ ---

Curry rice is a popular dish in Japan. It is made with curry sauce and rice. You can add meat and vegetables too.

--- ❈ ---

Mochi is a sweet rice cake in Japan. It is chewy and comes in many flavors. You can eat it as a snack or dessert.

Food and Cuisine

Dango are sweet rice dumplings in Japan. They are often served on skewers. You can eat them with sweet soy sauce or red bean paste.

--- ✤ ---

Taiyaki are fish-shaped cakes in Japan. They are filled with sweet red bean paste. You can find them at festivals and shops.

--- ✤ ---

Matcha is a type of green tea in Japan. It is bright green and has a strong flavor. You can drink it or use it in sweets.

Food and Cuisine

Tofu is a soft and white soybean curd. It is a popular ingredient in Japan. You can eat it in soups, stir-fries, and more.

Edamame are boiled and salted soybeans. They are a popular snack in Japan. You can eat them by squeezing the beans out of the pod.

Natto is a sticky and smelly soybean dish. It is very healthy and nutritious. You can eat it with rice and soy sauce.

Food and Cuisine

Yakisoba is a stir-fried noodle dish. It is made with noodles, meat, and vegetables. You can find it at festivals and markets.

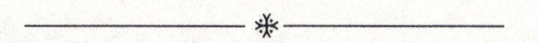

---- ❄ ----

Teriyaki is a sweet and salty sauce in Japan. It is used on grilled meats and fish. You can find it in many Japanese dishes.

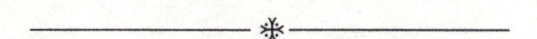

---- ❄ ----

Sukiyaki is a hot pot dish with thinly sliced beef. It is cooked at the table with vegetables and tofu. You can dip the meat in raw egg before eating.

Food and Cuisine

Shabu-shabu is a hot pot dish with thinly sliced meat. It is cooked quickly in boiling water. You can eat it with sauces and vegetables.

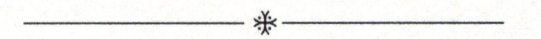

Yakiniku is a Japanese-style grilled dish where you cook meat and vegetables on a tabletop grill. It offers a fun and social dining experience.

Omurice is an omelette filled with fried rice. It is a popular dish in Japan. You can eat it with ketchup or a special sauce.

FESTIVALS AND CELEBRATIONS

Festivals and Celebrations

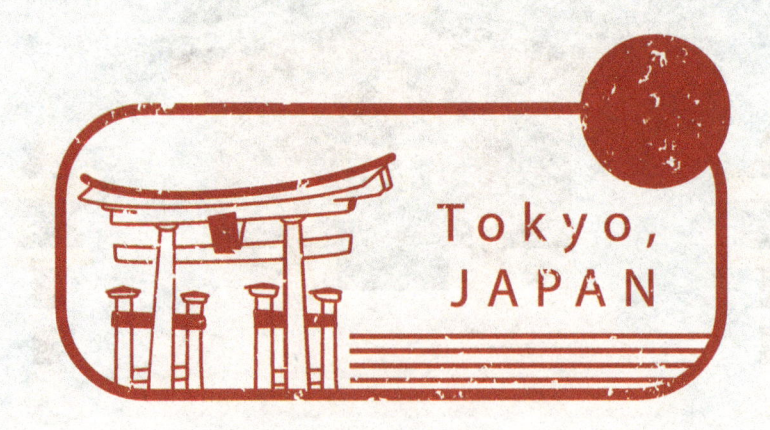

Tokyo, JAPAN

New Year is a big celebration in Japan. It lasts for several days. People visit shrines, eat special food, and send greeting cards.

---❉---

Hatsumode is the first visit to a shrine in the New Year. People pray for good luck and health. They also buy lucky charms and arrows.

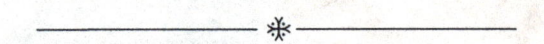

---❉---

Setsubun is a festival to celebrate the start of spring. It happens in February. People throw beans to chase away bad luck.

Festivals and Celebrations

Golden Week is a long holiday in Japan. It happens in late April and early May. People travel and visit family during this time.

---※---

Tanabata is a festival to celebrate two stars that meet once a year. It happens in July or August. People write wishes on paper and hang them on bamboo trees.

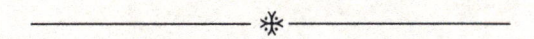

---※---

Obon is a festival to honor ancestors. It happens in the summer. People light lanterns and dance in special costumes.

Festivals and Celebrations

Tsukimi is a festival to look at the full moon. It happens in the fall. People eat special rice cakes and enjoy the moonlight.

The Lantern Festival is part of the Obon celebration. People light lanterns and float them on rivers. It is a beautiful and peaceful sight.

Setsubun is also called the Bean-Throwing Festival. People throw beans to chase away bad luck. They also eat sushi rolls and wear special masks.

Festivals and Celebrations

New Year's Eve is a special time in Japan. People eat soba noodles for good luck. They also listen to temple bells ring 108 times.

--- ❋ ---

Hatsuhinode is the first sunrise of the New Year. People wake up early to watch it. It brings good luck and a fresh start.

--- ❋ ---

Nengajo are special greeting cards sent during New Year's. They have pictures of the upcoming year's zodiac animal. People send them to friends and family.

Festivals and Celebrations

Culture Day is a holiday to celebrate culture in Japan. It happens in November. People visit museums and art galleries.

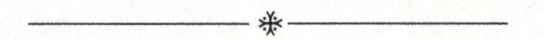

Mountain Day is a Japanese holiday dedicated to celebrating mountains. Observed in August, it encourages people to go hiking and appreciate nature.

Greenery Day is a holiday to celebrate nature in Japan. It happens in May. People plant trees and enjoy the outdoors.

Festivals and Celebrations

Showa Day is a holiday to celebrate the Showa era in Japan. It happens in April. People learn about history and remember the past.

---- ❉ ----

Health and Sports Day is a holiday to celebrate health and sports in Japan. It happens in October. People play sports and have parades.

---- ❉ ----

Fireworks Festivals are big celebrations in Japan. They happen in the summer. People watch fireworks and have picnics.

Festivals and Celebrations

Some towns celebrate Tanabata with vibrant parades featuring floats and music. Everyone joins in the festivities, dancing and singing, creating a lively and joyful atmosphere!

Tanabata festivals have lots of food stalls selling treats like candy apples and fried noodles. The yummy smells fill the air. It's like a carnival with stars as the theme!

Gion Matsuri in Kyoto is one of Japan's oldest festivals. It features huge, colorful floats pulled through the streets. It's like a moving museum!

Festivals and Celebrations

Awa Odori is a dance festival in August in Tokushima. Groups of dancers and musicians parade through the streets to lively traditional music. Spectators can join in the simple dance moves and chant along.

Hanafuda are special playing cards sometimes used in traditional games at New Year's. The cards are beautifully decorated with flowers and other nature motifs. People play games like koi-koi and hana-awase while snacking on New Year's treats.

Goldfish scooping, or kingyo sukui, is a popular game at summer festivals. Children try to scoop live goldfish into a bowl using a special paper scoop. If they can get a fish before the scoop breaks, they can take it home as a pet.

Festivals and Celebrations

Hagoita are decorative wooden paddles used in the traditional New Year's game hanetsuki. Adorned with images of kabuki actors or lucky symbols, they are sold as good luck charms and displayed in homes to bring fortune.

Washi paper is a traditional Japanese paper used to make all sorts of festival decorations. Lanterns, umbrellas, dolls, origami figures and more are crafted from the strong, translucent paper. Washi adds a delicate, timeless beauty to any celebration.

Kakigori is a treat that's especially popular at summer festivals - shaved ice topped with fruity or sweet syrups. The fluffy ice in a bowl or paper cup is the perfect way to cool down on a hot day. You can add extras like sweetened condensed milk or mochi balls.

Festivals and Celebrations

Ikebana is the Japanese art of flower arrangement, often used to decorate homes, public spaces and festival venues. Arrangements emphasize shape, line, form and empty space to create an artistic, balanced whole. Different styles and plants carry different meanings and emotions.

Temari are embroidered thread balls that were originally made from silk scraps and given to children to play with. Now they are decorative art pieces featuring intricate and colorful threaded patterns. Temari are sometimes displayed as ornaments during New Year's.

Matsuri bayashi is the traditional music played at festivals, usually by small ensembles. Musicians play flutes, shamisens, drums and bells in lively melodies over boisterous chanting and cheering. The music sets the tone for the festival's fun, celebratory atmosphere.

Festivals and Celebrations

Chochin are the paper lanterns that adorn festival grounds, often strung up along wires or in long chains. They create a soft, glowing ambiance and sometimes feature the name or symbol of the shrine or temple holding the festival. At the end of the festival, some people take lanterns home as souvenirs.

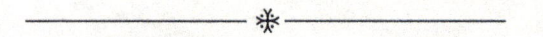

Yo-yo tsuri is a popular festival game that involves fishing for water balloons with a hook on a paper string. If you can hook a balloon and pull it up before the paper dissolves, you get to keep the balloon. It takes concentration and quick reflexes!

Furin are glass wind chimes tinkling with a pleasant sound thought to refresh the mind and spirit. They often feature a strip of paper with a poetic wish hanging down from the clapper. Furin are hung from the eaves of homes and shops in summer to welcome cool breezes and create a soothing atmosphere.

AMAZING ANIMALS OF JAPAN

Amazing Animals of Japan

The Red Fox is a clever and adaptable animal. It lives in many parts of Japan. Foxes are known for their beautiful red fur.

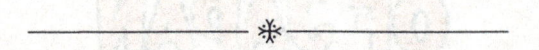

---------- ✹ ----------

Snow Monkeys is another name for Japanese Macaques. They have pink faces and grey fur. They are very cute and playful.

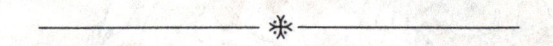

---------- ✹ ----------

The Tanuki is a species of raccoon dog that inhabits forests and mountains. Known for their playful and mischievous behavior, these creatures are a unique part of the ecosystem.

Amazing Animals of Japan

The Sika Deer is a beautiful and graceful animal. It lives in forests and grasslands. Sika Deer are known for their spotted fur.

The Japanese Squirrel is a small and cute animal. It lives in forests and parks. Squirrels are known for their bushy tails and quick movements.

Koi fish are colorful and often swim in ponds in Japan. They come in red, gold, white, and black patterns. It's like watching a rainbow underwater!

Amazing Animals of Japan

The Japanese pufferfish, known as fugu, is famous for being both adorable and dangerous. Its skin contains a poison that can be deadly to predators, making it like a spiky, hazardous balloon of the ocean!

---- ❋ ----

Wild boars, known as "inoshishi" in Japan, inhabit forests and mountains. They are powerful and swift runners, making them the athletes of the animal kingdom!

---- ❋ ----

The Japanese black bear is smaller than other bears and loves climbing trees. It's like the acrobat of the forest!

Amazing Animals of Japan

Japanese pond turtles are small and love swimming in rivers and ponds. They spend a lot of time basking in the sun on rocks. It's like they're tiny sunbathing pros!

---- ❄ ----

The Japanese serow is a goat-antelope that lives in the mountains. It has thick fur to stay warm in cold weather. It's like a mountain goat with a winter coat!

---- ❄ ----

The Japanese pheasant is the national bird of Japan. The males have shiny green feathers and bright red faces, making them very colorful. It's like they're wearing a fancy outfit!

Amazing Animals of Japan

The Japanese giant hornet is the largest hornet in the world. It can grow as long as a kid's pinky finger! It's like a flying superhero (or villain, depending on how you feel about bugs)!

--- ❋ ---

Japanese eels, called "unagi," live in rivers and lakes. They look like slippery snakes but are actually fish! It's like a long, wiggly ribbon in the water.

--- ❋ ---

Japanese river otters were once common in Japan's rivers. They loved playing in the water and eating fish. It's like they were the playful swimmers of the wild!

Amazing Animals of Japan

Japanese weasels are small, speedy hunters that live near rivers and forests. They have long, slim bodies and golden-brown fur. It's like they're tiny forest ninjas!

--- ❋ ---

The Japanese raven is a large, all-black bird with glossy feathers and a thick, curved beak. They are intelligent birds that can use tools to solve problems and find food. In Japanese culture, ravens are often seen as messengers of the gods.

--- ❋ ---

The Hokkaido fox, also known as the red fox, has reddish-brown fur and a fluffy tail. They are adaptable animals that can live in various habitats, from forests to urban areas. In Japanese folklore, foxes are depicted as clever and magical creatures.

Amazing Animals of Japan

The Japanese grosbeak is a large, stocky songbird with a thick, powerful beak. Males have pinkish-red feathers, while females are grayish-brown. These birds are known for their beautiful, warbling songs and are popular cage birds in Japan.

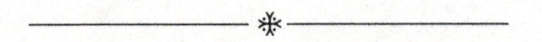

Japanese spider crabs have the longest leg span of any arthropod. Their bodies can reach 16 inches and their legs can reach 12 feet long! Spider crabs live in the waters around Japan.

Akita dogs are famous large, loyal Japanese dog breeds. Akitas have beautiful coats that can be red, white, or brindle. Akitas were originally used for hunting bears!

Amazing Animals of Japan

The Japanese dormouse, or aoko, is a small and adorable rodent species found in various habitats across Japan. These dormice are known for their cute appearance and their ability to go into a deep sleep, or torpor, during the winter months to conserve energy.

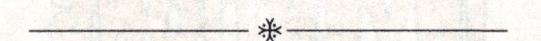

The Japanese pipistrelle bat, known as komuranezumi, is a small bat species crucial for controlling insect populations. These bats are agile flyers, adept at catching insects mid-flight, and are recognized for their high-pitched echolocation calls, which are nearly inaudible to humans.

The Japanese ibis, or toki, is a striking and beautiful bird species that was once on the brink of extinction. Thanks to conservation efforts, these birds have made a remarkable comeback and can now be seen in various parts of Japan. They are known for their distinctive curved beak and elegant plumage.

COOL JAPANESE INVENTIONS

Cool Japanese Inventions

Instant noodles were invented in Japan. They are quick to make and come in many flavors. Just add hot water and wait a few minutes.

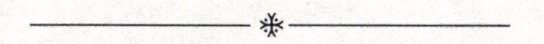

The first karaoke machine was made in Japan. It lets you sing along to your favorite songs. You can find them in many places, like bars and homes.

Japan has some of the fastest trains in the world. They are called bullet trains. These trains can go as fast as 320 km/h.

Cool Japanese Inventions

In Japan, many toilets are very advanced. They have buttons for different functions. Some can play music or make sounds to keep things private.

---- ❈ ----

Japan makes many friendly robots. They can help with tasks or just be friends. Some can even understand and talk to you.

---- ❈ ----

Bento boxes are a fun way to pack lunch. They come from Japan and have small sections for different foods. You can make them look like cute animals or characters.

Cool Japanese Inventions

Japan has cafes where you can play with cats. You pay to spend time with them. It's a fun way to relax with furry friends.

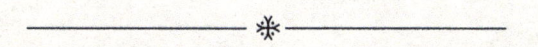

---　❋　---

Emojis were first used in Japan. They are small pictures you can use in messages. Now, people all over the world use them.

---　❋　---

QR codes are like barcodes that your phone can read. They were invented in Japan. You can scan them to get information quickly.

Cool Japanese Inventions

Sumo wrestling is a traditional sport in Japan. Wrestlers try to push each other out of a ring. They wear special belts and follow old rules.

Kimono is a traditional clothing in Japan. It's a long robe with wide sleeves. You wear it with a belt called an obi.

Koto is a traditional instrument from Japan. It has 13 strings and is played with picks on your fingers. You can hear it in classical music.

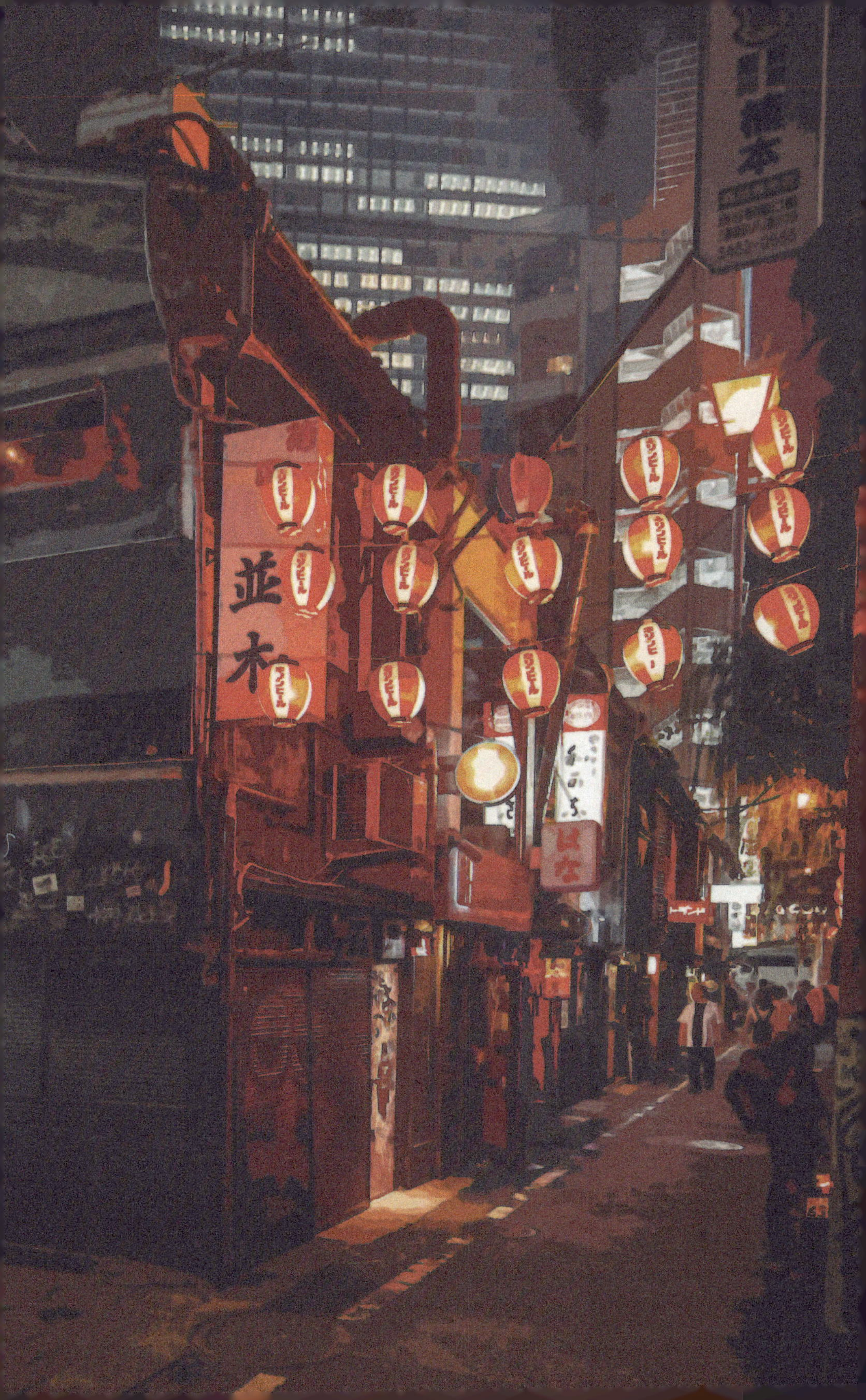
並木

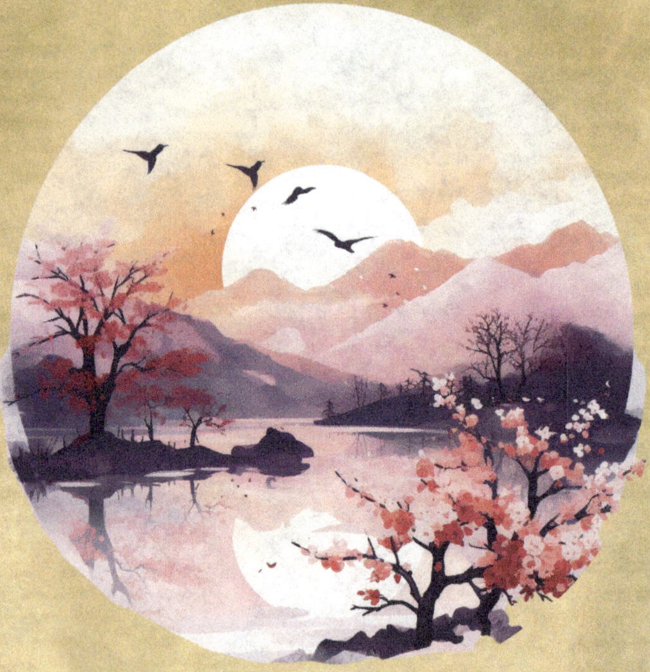

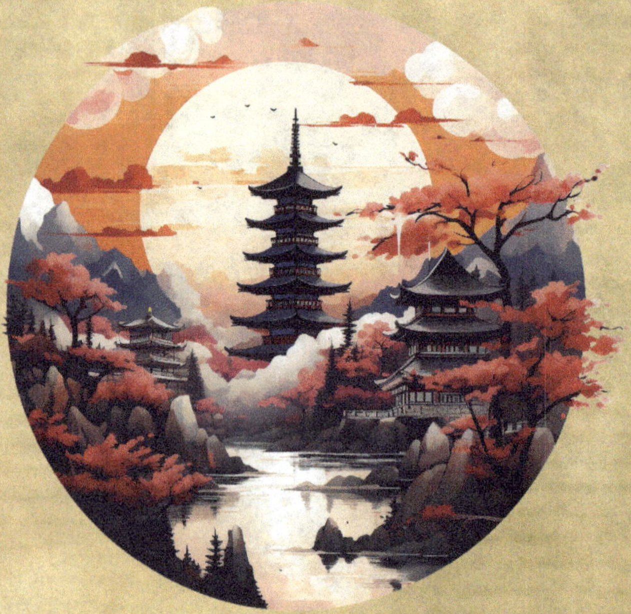

83

84

85

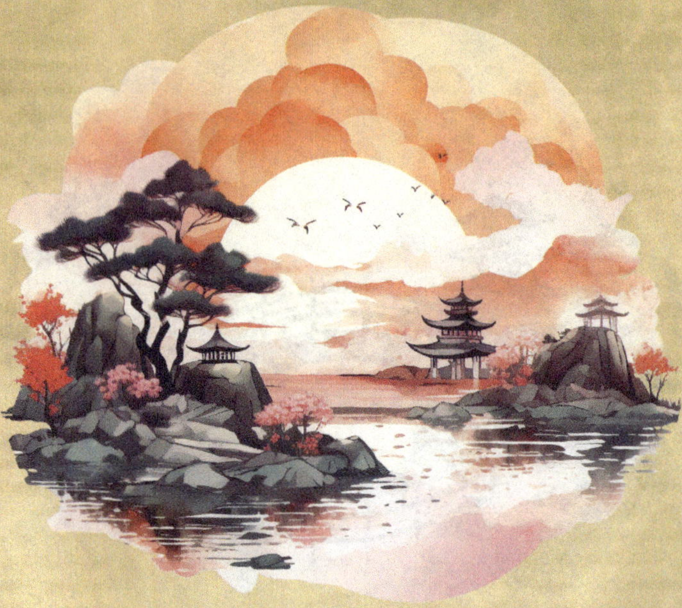

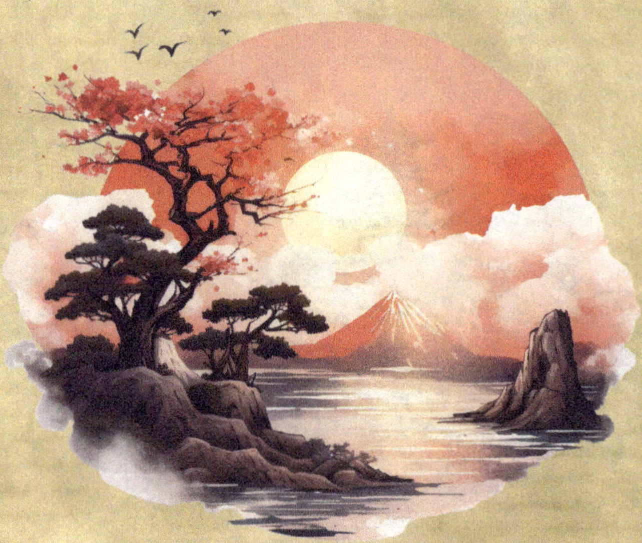

Made in the USA
Monee, IL
13 March 2025